CAPTURED
HISTORY

HITLER IN PARIS

HOW A PHOTOGRAPH SHOCKED A WORLD AT WAR

by Don Nardo

Content Adviser: Arnold Krammer, PhD
Professor of History
Texas A&M University

COMPASS POINT BOOKS
a capstone imprint

Compass Point Books are published by Capstone,
1710 Roe Crest Drive, North Mankato, Minnesota 56003
www.capstonepub.com

Editor: Catherine Neitge
Designer: Tracy Davies McCabe
Media Researcher: Svetlana Zhurkin
Library Consultant: Kathleen Baxter
Production Specialist: Kathy McColley

Image Credits
Alamy: DIZ Muenchen GmbH/Sueddeutsche Zeitung Photo, 11, 38, 40; Corbis, 47;
DVIC/NARA, cover, 12, 31, 33, 57 (top); Getty Images: Galerie Bilderwelt, 17, Time
Life Pictures/George Lacks, 32, Time Life Pictures/Heinrich Hoffmann, 8; Library
of Congress, 16, 19, 23, 25, 42, 49, 54, 56, 57 (bottom), 58, 59; Newscom: akg-
images, 5, 7, 21, 27, 29, 37, 44, picture alliance/Archiv/Berliner Verlag, 35, Picture
History, 15, ZUMA Press/Keystone Pictures USA, 50; Sergey Larenkov, 53

Library of Congress Cataloging-in-Publication Data
Nardo, Don, 1947–
Hitler in Paris: how a photograph shocked a world at war / by Don Nardo.
pages cm.—(Captured history)
Audience: Grade 4 to 6.
Includes bibliographical references and index.
ISBN 978-0-7565-4733-2 (library binding)
ISBN 978-0-7565-4789-9 (paperback)
ISBN 978-0-7565-4795-0 (ebook PDF)
1. Hitler, Adolf, 1889–1945—Pictorial works—Juvenile literature. 2. Hitler,
Adolf, 1889–1945—Travel—France—Paris—Juvenile literature. 3. Tour Eiffel
(Paris, France)—Pictorial works—Juvenile literature. 4. Photographs—Political
aspects—History—20th century—Juvenile literature. 5. World War, 1939–1945—
Photography—Juvenile literature. 6. World War, 1939–1945—France—Paris—
Juvenile literature. 7. Paris (France)—History, Military—20th century—Juvenile
literature. 8. France—History—German occupation, 1940–1945—Juvenile
literature. I. Title.
DD247.H5N36 2014
943.086092—dc23   2013030415

Printed in the United States of America in Stevens Point, Wisconsin.
092013   007773WZS14

TABLEOFCONTENTS

ChapterOne
AN EARLY MORNING IN PARIS

It was nearly 5:30 in the morning of June 28, 1940. A dim deep-orange predawn glow hung above the eastern horizon. The nighttime runway lights, intended to guide planes to safe landings in the dark, were still lit at Paris' Le Bourget airport. A handful of airfield ground crew members waited on the tarmac. Watching them closely were several dozen well-armed German soldiers.

A few minutes later, all present heard the distant drone of an approaching plane's engines. Scanning the sky, they made out its lights and watched as it descended. After landing smoothly, the aircraft taxied to the terminal. Some of the German soldiers hurried over and stood guard over a small group of men getting off the plane. Without fanfare, the new arrivals walked to three waiting Mercedes sedans.

Ten minutes later, the cars, their headlights still on, motored quietly through the streets of one of Paris' large suburbs. Among the passengers was a 54-year-old German photographer, Heinrich Hoffmann. According to an acquaintance, he was "a short, comfortably tubby little man … with a pair of bright, merry, and quickly twinkling eyes." Hoffmann, then Germany's most commercially successful photographer, had the hands "of an artist," the acquaintance recalled.

Accompanying Hoffmann were other notable German

A Nazi flag flying from the Arc de Triomphe was a constant reminder of the German occupation of Paris.

artistic figures. One was the bold and talented architect Albert Speer. Also present was fellow architect Hermann Giessler and the noted German sculptor Arno Breker.

A fifth man rode with the others. Both outside and inside the cars, Hoffmann and the others showed unusual respect for him. There was good reason. He was Germany's reigning dictator and head of the Nazi regime that controlled their country.

Adolf Hitler, like his personal photographer, Heinrich Hoffmann, was short—about 5-foot-8 (173 centimeters). Unlike Hoffmann, however, Hitler was physically unattractive. He was painfully aware that his nose was too big for his face. He tried to offset it by wearing a narrow but bushy mustache, which remained his signature for the rest of his life.

Added to Hitler's physical quirks were some odd and at times frightening personality traits. He had a terrible temper, which made him prone to violent tantrums. At times he displayed a warped sense of humor. He often poked fun at deaf people and amputees. A more developed aspect of this cruel streak was his deep hatred of people of certain races and ethnic groups. At the top of his hate list were Jews. But he abhorred Slavs, blacks, nomadic people called Gypsies, and many others nearly as much.

Hitler's negative traits made him physically unimpressive and at times repulsive or even scary to be around. Yet he also had qualities that had plainly helped him achieve his success as a national leader. Hoffmann,

Hitler's negative traits made him physically unimpressive and at times repulsive or even scary to be around.

Heinrich Hoffmann (far right) with Adolf Hitler (third from left) and Hitler's staff in June 1940

who knew him for more than 20 years, called him "a charming and witty conversationalist." Hitler also had a striking intensity and zeal for certain ideas, projects, and goals. He was known to home in on a problem and relentlessly pursue a solution.

Hitler also showed a tremendous confidence in himself. This stemmed from his view that he was meant to play a key role in humanity's destiny. "Hitler firmly believed that he had been chosen by Fate," Hoffmann later wrote, "to lead the German people to hitherto undreamed of heights; and his rise to power" as dictator of Germany

Hoffmann's camera captured an enthusiastic crowd saluting Hitler in 1936.

"only strengthened this belief." So whether one liked or disliked Hitler, his all-consuming passion for his interests and beliefs, combined with his power as dictator, made him impossible to ignore.

Hitler had an uncanny ability to make other people share his interests and beliefs. He was able to sway a crowd in ways that most public speakers could only dream about. This talent had helped him to manipulate the German people during the 1920s and 1930s. He convinced them that he could solve their problems, and with their backing he cleverly used the nation's political system to obtain absolute power.

Once he had gained supreme authority, however, Hitler ruled through brutal means. His words, and even his whims, carried the force of law. Few people dared to object, and those who did were severely beaten or murdered. His control over society was so total that he personally dictated the standards for literature, architecture, sculpture, and music. He even decided "the colors artists could use in paintings," Williams College professor Robert Waite wrote. Also up to him were "the way lobsters were to be cooked in restaurants, and how physics would be taught in the universities. He decided whom Germans might marry, what they could name their children, where they could be buried," Waite wrote. "At his command thousands of young soldiers died in hopeless battle, many with his name on their lips. On his orders millions of people were tortured, maimed, murdered."

Hitler became so powerful, esteemed, and feared that most Germans called him simply the Führer, meaning "great leader." His sweeping authority was mostly based on his command of Germany's extensive armed forces. They had recently swept into Poland, starting a conflict that would soon become known as World War II.

Next Hitler's lethal war machine had smashed its way into western Europe and invaded Germany's longtime archenemy, France. Only 22 years earlier, France and the other Allies had defeated Germany in World War I (1914–1918). Now the tables were turned. Germany invaded France, and unprepared for the onslaught,

> **Few people dared to object, and those who did were severely beaten or murdered.**

French defenses had crumbled. With nothing to stop them, thousands of German troops had entered Paris on June 14, 1940, an event that had shocked the world. To make sure none of the Parisians doubted they were beaten, German soldiers climbed to the top of the famous Eiffel Tower. There they unfurled the Nazis' red and black flag, bearing their dreaded symbol—the swastika.

Excited over his triumph, Hitler decided to visit the French capital. He ruled out staging a victory parade. That, he reasoned, would come later. Instead the visit would be short, quiet, and discreet. An avid lover of large-scale architecture, he strongly desired to see Parisian landmarks. In particular, he was eager to tour the city's renowned opera house, the Palais Garnier. Like many other tourists, he also wanted to ride to the top of the Eiffel Tower.

Hitler took along Hoffmann to document the trip in photos. This was nothing new. Hoffmann followed the Nazi leader almost everywhere, snapping dozens of pictures at each stop or event. As a historian put it, Hitler saw Hoffmann as "his court photographer, the only man who for years was permitted to photograph him." The outing to Paris was an experience that Germany's dictator especially wanted to record for posterity. His tours of the opera house and other significant architectural buildings and monuments were important to him. He wanted to have pictures of the visit that he could fondly examine later.

More important, Hitler wanted photos of the visit

FAVORITE ARTISTS

Hitler and staff visit La Madeleine, a landmark Paris church originally designed as a temple to the glory of Napoleon's army. Hitler is flanked (from left) by Hermann Giessler, Albert Speer, and Arno Breker.

On his short but historic trip to Paris, Hitler took along three of his favorite artists—Albert Speer, Hermann Giessler, and Arno Breker. Speer (1905–1981) was Germany's most renowned architect during the Nazi era. He also served as Hitler's minister of armaments and war production. During World War II, at Hitler's request, Speer prepared elaborate plans to create a new, much larger and grander Berlin, featuring several enormous government structures. Thanks to Nazi Germany's collapse in 1944–45, these were never built. After the war, Speer served 20 years in prison for his involvement in Hitler's regime.

Giessler (1898–1987) was a German architect whom Hitler ranked second only to Speer. Hitler hired Giessler to design and build his house in Munich. Later Hitler ordered him to reorganize the Austrian city of Linz. Giessler was sentenced to life in prison after the war but was released in 1952.

Breker (1900–1991) became Hitler's favorite sculptor in the 1930s and soon enjoyed the status of the Nazi regime's official sculptor. Among Breker's most renowned works were large statues carved for the summer Olympic Games in Berlin in 1936. After the war Breker was merely fined and allowed to continue working.

In a photo that would send a chill throughout the world, Adolf Hitler poses in front of the Eiffel Tower with Albert Speer (left) and Arno Breker.

for propaganda purposes. It was his first visit to France's leading city after the nation's fall to German forces. He calculated, quite correctly, that photos showing him standing before renowned Parisian landmarks would be enormously powerful. They would trumpet his great victory to people across the globe.

Hoffmann proceeded to take the photos needed to do that. Two pictures in particular—both showing Hitler with the Eiffel Tower behind him—shocked and worried Germany's adversaries. Making it worse, images showing one of history's cruelest dictators in front of the enduring symbol of a free, democratic people were jarring and disturbing. Even after many decades, they remain so.

Chapter Two

MAKING HISTORY ALMOST DAILY

Adolf Hitler was one of the most photographed people in history. Heinrich Hoffmann's images of him number more than 2 million. Hundreds of other photographers, from Germany and many other nations, also captured Hitler's likeness. Some of these artists were filmmakers. The most famous of their number was an award-winning German actress and movie director, Leni Riefenstahl.

Hoffmann, along with Riefenstahl, "did more to promote Adolf Hitler than any of the other Nazi propagandists," according to Professor Steven Heller of New York's School of Visual Arts.

Hoffmann and Riefenstahl were both on hand for one of the most memorable of Hitler's many photo sessions. It took place at a Nazi rally in September 1934 on the parade grounds at Nuremberg, in south-central Germany. The huge rally was the second of its kind after Hitler became Germany's chancellor, the head of the government's executive branch, in January 1933. A crowd of more than 1 million, many wearing swastika-decorated armbands, turned out to hear the Nazi leader speak.

Hoffmann hurried to and fro during the speech and other festivities. He snapped his camera shutter so many times that his fingers grew numb. Meanwhile, Riefenstahl and her cameramen shot the footage she needed for a documentary film of the event. Titled *Triumph of the Will,*

Hitler arrives to speak at a huge Nazi rally in Nuremberg in 1934.

it was released in 1936. It was shown in movie theaters across Germany and, in a masterstroke of propaganda, it was given free to be shown in France.

American journalist William L. Shirer was also at the rally. He was stunned by the dramatic sweep of the event. Yet he was also troubled by the excessive adulation heaped on Hitler by the Germans who were there. "I got caught in a mob of ten thousand hysterics," Shirer later wrote, "who jammed the moat in front of Hitler's hotel, shouting: 'We want our Führer!' I was a little shocked at the faces,

Adoring German
farm girls reach
out to touch Nazi
leader Hitler
in 1935.

especially those of the women, when Hitler finally appeared on the balcony for a moment. ... They looked up at him as if he were a Messiah, their faces transformed into something positively inhuman."

Unlike the enthralled fans, many of whom *did* see Hitler as a kind of god, Hoffmann viewed him as quite human. To the photographer, the Nazi leader was foremost an employer who recognized Hoffmann's gift for capturing on film the drama of historic events. For this Hoffmann was very grateful. Hitler saw Hoffmann as a talented artist whose photos effectively documented the Third Reich, the Nazi government.

Hoffmann, Eva Braun, and Hitler look over Hoffmann's photos at the Berghof, the Nazi leader's retreat near Berchtesgaden, Germany.

Hitler and Hoffmann, therefore, were a team. On a personal level, they got along well in part because Hoffmann had introduced his boss to Eva Braun. A native of Munich, she was working as Hoffmann's assistant and model at age 17 when she first met Hitler. About two years later, she became the Nazi leader's permanent girlfriend. Hitler always remained grateful to Hoffmann for bringing Braun into his life.

The photographer and the Führer also got along well because both loved the arts and enjoyed discussing them. Professionally speaking, the partnership was successful because each made history almost every day. Hitler's short but historic trip to Paris, and Hoffmann's iconic photos of the event, are a vivid example of that.

In spite of their personal and professional relationships, however, the two men were very different. Hitler had a dark, tortured personality. He was self-centered, obsessive, mean-spirited, and power-hungry. Hoffmann was easygoing, good-natured, and generous. He had no interest in acquiring power over others. He only wanted to practice his craft to the best of his ability. A look at their lives before the Paris trip shows what made them so different.

Hitler was born April 20, 1889, in the obscure Austrian hamlet of Braunau am Inn. His father, Alois Hitler, was a lower-middle-class customs official. The father and son did not get along. From an early age, Adolf was an average student but showed an interest in becoming an artist. His father sternly rejected the idea. When the boy protested, he was beaten with a horsewhip. Alois Hitler died in 1903, leaving his 13-year-old son hugely relieved.

Adolf enjoyed a close relationship with his mother, Klara Hitler. At times she spoiled him to help make up for her husband's cruelty. The young man's pleasant times with his mother did not last long, however. He was devastated when she died of breast cancer in 1907.

Adolf Hitler (top right) as a young student in Austria in 1901

The family doctor later recalled, "In all my career, I never saw anyone so prostrate with grief as Adolf Hitler."

In his teens and early 20s, Hitler avidly read about Germany's past. Though born in Austria, he was one of many Austrians who felt that their land had always been part of Germany and would be again. He enjoyed books about the medieval Teutonic knights. These tall, blond men were said to have performed heroic deeds. They were supposedly members of a superior race, the Aryans. There was no such race. But Hitler thought it had been real. Moreover, he believed that Germans were the Aryans' direct descendants.

Despite his vivid imagination, Hitler did not do well in high school, and he dropped out at age 16. He spent his time reading, drawing, and painting. In 1908, when he was 19, he applied to a famous arts academy in Austria's capital, Vienna. He was rejected. The instructors felt he lacked the talent needed to become a good painter. Disappointed and disgruntled, he worked at odd jobs for a few years and was sometimes reduced to living on the streets, blaming others for his failures.

Throughout Hitler's period of drifting through a largely unhappy life, he was learning to hate. He read and absorbed a great deal of anti-Jewish literature and developed a strong, irrational hatred for Jews. In one of his earliest anti-Semitic essays, he accused them of being racially impure and greedy for money. In general, he wrote, they "produce a racial tuberculosis among nations."

Thus Hitler was a sour, discontented racist even before a terrible war erupted and made him even worse. When World War I began in 1914, he was 25, and he enlisted in the German army. He became a courier and performed bravely, carrying messages from trench to trench. He saw fighting against the British and suffered from the effects of poison gas, winning an Iron Cross, First Class, medal.

During the war years, Hitler never asked to go on leave. When he was off duty, he reportedly would often sit alone in a corner for long periods. "Suddenly," a fellow soldier

Throughout
Hitler's period
of drifting
through
a largely
unhappy
life, he was
learning
to hate.

Hitler (right) with a fellow soldier during World War I

later remembered, "he would leap up and, running about excitedly, say that in spite of our big guns victory would be denied us, for the invisible foes of the German people were a greater danger than the biggest cannon of the enemy."

Among the enemies the increasingly paranoid Hitler imagined were the Jews. Over time, he would add communists, big bankers, and others to his hate list. Hitler, along with many of his countrymen, blamed these "degenerate" elements of German society for his country's defeat in World War I.

In reality, Germany's incompetent generals were the guilty parties. But this was extremely difficult for most Germans to accept. As a historian points out, they had grown up having immense respect, even a reverence, for their military forces. As a result, he wrote, they "could not grasp the fact that their armies had lost the war."

The loss humiliated Hitler and other Germans to their core. In addition, the 1919 Treaty of Versailles imposed very harsh terms on Germany. Embittered, many Germans were open to accepting a myth that Hitler and his followers advanced. According to the myth, Germany had been the victim of a "stab in the back." It held that certain groups at home, rather than the generals, had caused the defeat. Liberal politicians, communists, Jews, and big bankers had betrayed the country, the story went. Although untrue, the myth soon became an article of faith among most Germans.

The myth also helped to make the reputation of Adolf Hitler, who had been an unknown politician. In 1920 he

Hitler posed for Hoffmann's camera upon his release from Landesberg Prison.

helped turn the small German Workers' Party into an important political force. It became the National Socialist German Workers Party—the Nazi Party, for short.

Partly because Hitler was so effective at public speaking, the group grew swiftly. But there were ups and downs along the way. In 1923, for example, the Nazis attempted a coup against the government of the state of Bavaria. It failed, and Hitler was sentenced to five years in prison. Yet the setback ended up making the chief Nazi and his movement stronger. Winning early release, he served only nine months of his sentence.

Also, while in his cell, he wrote the first volume of *Mein Kampf (My Struggle)*. The book's summary of Hitler's bizarre, paranoid beliefs and its promises that he would make Germany great strongly appealed to many unhappy people. It did not sell well at first, but once Hitler came to power, it sold millions of copies.

Thereafter, the Führer, as his followers had come to call him, gained increasing public respect and support. This allowed him to use mostly legal means to achieve power. In the July 1932 national election, for instance, the Nazis won an impressive 40 percent of the seats in Germany's parliament, the Reichstag. Even though their numbers dropped considerably in the November elections, Hitler was appointed chancellor in 1933. That allowed him to push through a series of laws that gave him dictatorial powers. In very short order, he turned Germany into a police state. Anyone who was caught speaking out against the Nazis was brutally beaten or jailed or both.

Even as Hitler was transforming Germany, his larger goal—to dominate all of Europe and beyond—was becoming apparent. In 1935 he started to rearm the country. This violated the 1919 Versailles Treaty, which ended World War I. More ominously, he signed a pact in 1936 with Italy's right-wing dictator, Benito Mussolini. Nazi Germany and Fascist Italy were fighting on the same side during the Spanish Civil War (1936–1939).

Hitler and Mussolini's creation of the so-called Berlin-Rome Axis troubled many British, French, and American leaders. But they did not interfere. Winston

Anyone who was caught speaking out against the Nazis was brutally beaten or jailed or both.

A 1936 portrait of Hitler, one of many taken by Hoffmann, his personal photographer

Churchill, Britain's renowned statesman, later recalled this terribly unwise decision. Allowing Hitler "to rearm without active interference by the Allies," Churchill said, made a new world war "almost certain." He added, "Hitler was now free to strike," and "almost all that remained open to France and Britain was to await the moment of the challenge and do the best they could."

That moment came September 1, 1939. Hitler's now vast and lethal forces swept into and captured Poland, setting World War II in motion. Just a few months later, early in 1940, German soldiers poured into Norway, Denmark, Belgium, and Holland. It was clear that France would be Hitler's next target, and sure enough, German troops entered France in May. On June 5 enormous numbers of German troops launched an assault. In journalist Shirer's words, they "surged across France like a tidal wave."

The leaders of the French government hastily fled Paris on June 10. Four days later the German army entered the undefended city. Hitler had achieved much of his long-awaited revenge on the French. The way was now clear for him to receive their surrender. He also looked forward to visiting Paris, whose cultural treasures he now viewed as his personal possessions.

Heinrich Hoffmann reached Paris in June 1940 by quite a different route. Like Hitler, Hoffmann hailed from middle-class origins. He too had steadily risen to prominence in German society. But Hoffmann had done it considerably faster than Hitler had. Hoffmann was "remarkable in both character and experience," in the view of a scholar who came to know him after the war.

One major reason that Hoffmann gained so much success in photography was that he learned the craft from his father. Heinrich Hoffmann was born September 12, 1885, in Fürth, a town in Bavaria. As he grew up, his father worked as a court photographer for Bavaria's royal family. Heinrich apprenticed with his father and later worked with him in a family-run portrait studio in the Bavarian city of Munich.

One major reason that Hoffmann gained so much success in photography was that he learned the craft from his father.

MEANT TO BE A PHOTOGRAPHER?

A photograph of Hitler by Hoffmann appeared on a photo postcard.

A major reason that Heinrich Hoffmann so willingly worked for Hitler was that the dictator gave Hoffmann a large-scale outlet for his talents as a photographer. And Hoffmann felt he was born to be both an artist and a photographer. In his autobiography, *Hitler Was My Friend* (one of several books he wrote about Hitler), Hoffmann said, "By profession, I have always been a photographer. And by inclination a passionate devotee of the arts, a publisher of art journals, and a devout, if modest, wielder of pencil and brush."

With his high-quality, German-made Leica 35mm camera, Hoffmann took full advantage of Hitler's patronage. The two men were greatly pleased with the photos Hoffmann took, and they benefited financially from them. Germans and foreigners bought vast numbers of copies of many of Hoffmann's pictures. This made both men millionaires in an era in which the average German worker earned $1,500 a year and someone who made $5,000 a year was considered well-to-do.

As the young man matured, he steadily outdid his father in some areas of their trade. More than most other photographers of his day, Heinrich Hoffmann saw that picture-making could and should go beyond portraits and other posed pictures. In particular, he recognized the power of capturing notable people and events in a candid way, as they happened. These would give the public and future generations a good idea of what the people and events were like.

In his 20s and 30s, he used his talent to good advantage. He worked with some of the best photographers in Germany and learned as much as possible from them. They introduced him to rich and famous people. As a result, he took pictures of many celebrities, especially musicians, actors, painters, and other artists. "In the artistic field, my contacts were numerous indeed," he later recalled. "At one time or another, all the famous stars of theater and music ... posed for my camera." Other notables Hoffmann immortalized in photos included high-ranking military officers and Germany's leader, Kaiser Wilhelm II.

Producing such portraits brought Hoffmann considerable fame. But his greatest early success came from his photography of dramatic unexpected events. In one case, a "shattering explosion," in his words, occurred near where he was working. "I snatched up my camera and rushed out into the open into the midst of an appalling panic." A large observation balloon had crashed and blown up. "The dead lay mingled with the wounded,

Portraits of Hitler filled the windows of Hoffmann's shop in a snapshot from Eva Braun's photo album.

bloody, groaning, and writhing on the ground," he later remembered. "Setting up my camera, I swiftly took pictures of the disaster." Newspapers bought the photos to illustrate articles, and he recalled that the pictures "caused a sensation. By chance, I had beaten all my competitors by miles!"

Photographing breaking news events made Hoffmann a great deal of money. "Very few photographers had had the [toughness] to stand in the midst of [dangerous situations] to take snaps," he explained. "My photos, therefore, were in many ways unique, and consequently they fetched high prices."

At the time, of course, Hoffmann had no inkling that capturing breaking news events for Hitler would eventually occupy almost all his time. He first saw the Nazi leader in 1920 at a street rally in Munich. "Among other speakers," Hoffmann later wrote, "was one Adolf Hitler. I saw no reason for wasting a [photographic] plate on this nonentity."

Two more years passed before Hoffmann met the man he had assumed was not worth wasting film on. An American newspaper offered him $100 to make a portrait of Hitler. Considering that the standard fee then for such pictures was just $5, it was a deal Hoffmann could not pass up. In the midst of his attempt to get the shot of Hitler, the two men had a long conversation. It ended with Hitler exclaiming, "Herr Hoffmann, I like you!"

It was not long before Hitler asked Hoffmann to become his official photographer, and Hoffmann accepted. Decades later someone asked him why he got along so well with Hitler, who had committed so many crimes against humanity. "My friendship with Hitler was a purely personal relationship," Hoffmann replied. "It was my continued lack of interest in politics, in power or in position ... that caused him to give [his] confidence to a man who, he well knew, had no personal axe to grind and would talk frankly and freely to him."

Hoffmann seems to have been one of only a handful of people who could criticize a Nazi policy to Hitler's face and live to tell the tale. When the Nazis began burning books in public in the 1930s, for example, the photographer said he confronted Hitler. "Things like that," Hoffmann said, "merely bring the Reich and the

Hoffmann seems to have been one of only a handful of people who could criticize a Nazi policy to Hitler's face and live to tell the tale.

University students across Germany, including thousands in Berlin, burned "un-German" books.

Party into disrepute. [And] all they accomplish is to raise a few cheap cheers from the mob and rabble."

Hoffmann recalled that Hitler said he agreed with him in principle, but unfortunately such things were necessary. To someone else on a separate occasion, Hitler explained why. After calling most of his countrymen stupid and lazy, he is reported to have said that "cruelty is impressive. Cruelty and brutal strength. ... The masses want it. They need the thrill of terror to make them shudderingly submissive." He added, "Terror is the most effective way of politics."

Hitler rarely showed the darker aspects of his personality to Hoffmann. It is possible that Hitler acted

like a reasonable person around the photographer in order to maintain his loyalty. Hitler recognized Hoffmann's singular ability to capture the pageantry of the Third Reich on film.

Hoffmann's loyalty and talent paid off repeatedly for Hitler. The 1934 Nuremberg rally was only one of many large-scale Nazi events that Hoffmann covered in the 1930s. He comprehensively and brilliantly documented them, serving as the official Nazi photographer for books, postcards, and other propaganda materials.

The outbreak of World War II and France's fall spawned events on an even larger scale. Hitler now looked

forward to making history in two places on French soil. The
first would be the spot where he would, with great relish,
receive the surrender of his most hated enemy. The second
place would be France's capital, where he would flaunt
his electrifying victory to people across the globe. These
would be his greatest accomplishments to date, he knew.
Hitler also realized that at this moment he needed Heinrich
Hoffmann at his side more than ever. Hoffmann's keen eye
and trusty camera lens would be needed to record the most
dramatic moments of Hitler's life.

ChapterThree
REVENGE ON FRANCE COMPLETE

Adolf Hitler was in his western headquarters near Brussels, Belgium, when he received the electrifying news that France had fallen. Throughout most of his adult life, he had passionately hated that neighbor of Germany. His mind harkened back to the dark days at the close of World War I. In his mind the "stab in the back" at home had been equaled by the arrogance of the French leaders when the Treaty of Versailles was created after Germany lost the war. France and the other Allies had also humiliated the German generals, he believed. They had been forced to sign the surrender document in a small railway car on the edge of the forest at Compiègne, not far northeast of Paris. Thereafter, the German people had suffered through years of economic turmoil and second-class status as a nation.

Now, finally, Hitler would enjoy the vengeance he had long dreamed of. He would force the French to sign their own humiliating surrender. He would also visit France's capital, Paris, at his leisure. His presence there would further rub French noses into the degrading dirt of defeat.

All of these things and more seem to have exploded in Hitler's consciousness when he learned of his victory over the French. One of his leading officers, Field Marshal Wilhelm Keitel, was with him. So was Heinrich Hoffmann, standing quietly behind the military men. The photographer later remembered the Nazi leader's

German tanks rolled into Rouen in northern France in June 1940.

immediate reaction to the news. "For a moment he threw to the winds his dignity as Supreme Commander of the Armed Forces and slapped himself gleefully on the thigh. And it was then that Keitel, carried away by this burst of emotion, coined the fateful phrase 'Mein Führer, you are the greatest military commander of all time!'"

Almost immediately, the ecstatic Hitler began planning the armistice signing between himself and the French.

He had hatched a plan designed to inflict a maximum of embarrassment and shame on his defeated enemies. The surrender would take place in the same railway car in which the earlier document had been signed. To add insult to injury, the car would sit on the exact spot it had occupied in 1918. This required that the vehicle be moved from the Compiègne museum. So Hitler ordered wrecking crews to tear down one of the building's walls. Laborers removed the railway car and brought it to the place where the World War I armistice had occurred.

All was ready, therefore, for Hitler to exact part of his revenge on France. Heinrich Hoffmann was with him on the big day—June 21, 1940. They sat together in Hitler's Mercedes as it and other cars carrying Nazi officials headed for the armistice site. Just before their arrival, the photographer turned to Hitler and said, "This place has become a sort of historical pilgrim center for the French." Many of them, he added, buy "postcards and colored pictures of the signing of the armistice of 1918!"

Hitler normally became upset when someone mentioned Germany's surrender in 1918. But this time was different, for he was now the victor. Also, Hoffmann was nonpolitical and harmless. So he could be forgiven for making inappropriate remarks now and then. Shrugging, Hitler responded, "I don't blame the French for that. But now it's our turn." At that moment, the car was stopping near the armistice site. "Hoffmann!" the Nazi leader called out. "Come on, let's get on with it!"

Hoffmann captured a photo of Hitler arriving at Compiègne to exact his revenge.

The men got out of the cars at 3:15 p.m. and headed toward the railway car. On the way, they walked proudly in front of an honor guard of German soldiers. American reporter William Shirer was one of the many foreign journalists covering the epic event. He studied the Nazi leaders, and in particular the famous Hitler. "I observed his face," Shirer later wrote in his diary. "It was grave, solemn, yet brimming with revenge. There was also in it, as in his springy step, a note of the triumphant conqueror, the defier of the world. There was something else ... a sort

With the railway car in the background, Hitler walked past German soldiers at Compiègne.

of scornful, inner joy at being present at this great reversal of fate—a reversal he himself had wrought."

As the afternoon wore on, the tireless Hoffmann snapped photo after photo. He knew it was vital that his camera not miss any of the historic moments of the event. Hoffmann took shots of the German and French delegations standing outside the railway car. He also snapped many photos of the signing ceremony inside.

After some discussion and other minor delays, the parties signed the treaty shortly before 7 o'clock. An important part of Hitler's revenge on France was now complete. But for him, the sweetest part was yet to come. The next day he summoned his chief architect, Albert Speer, to his headquarters in Belgium. "In a few days we are flying to Paris," Hitler told Speer. "I'd like you to be with us. Breker and Giessler are coming along also."

Speer later said he was "astonished that the victor had sent for three artists to accompany him on his entry into the French capital." He continued, "This was not to be an official visit, I learned, but a kind of 'art tour' by Hitler. This was the city, as he had so often said, which had fascinated him from his earliest years." Hitler "thought he would be able to find his way about the streets and important monuments, as if he had lived there, solely from his endless studies of its plans."

The Paris tour began early in the morning of June 28. After arriving at the airport, Hitler, the three artists, and Heinrich Hoffmann were driven straight to the Paris Opera. Hitler had long admired the architecture of Europe's opera houses. This one was by far his favorite. "That is my opera house!" he told the other men. "From my earliest youth, it has been my dream to gaze upon this magnificent example of French architectural genius!"

Hoffmann later recalled, "War, power, politics— everything was forgotten. And he went through the building as if he were determined to carry every little corner in his memory forever." The photographer took several shots inside the building. One showed Hitler and

Hitler and his group left the Paris Opera on their way to the Eiffel Tower.

the three Nazi artists standing at the top of the lobby's massive winding staircase.

From there the men moved on to the world-famous Eiffel Tower. Hitler very much desired to ride to the top. But he was told that French patriots had tampered with the elevator mechanism. He would have had to climb all 1,710 steps to the top. He decided against it because he lacked both the time and energy for such a feat.

However, Hitler made sure the famous structure shared the spotlight with him in two of Hoffmann's photos. One shows Hitler standing in the foreground with the tower behind him. Speer stands to his right and Breker to his left. Visible at lower right is a filmmaker, camera in hand, shooting live footage of the momentous scene. In the other photo, Speer, Breker, Giessler, and Hitler, with members of his senior staff, walk together. Again the Nazi leader is in the center and the tower looms behind them.

Hitler realized how important it was to pose himself with the grand structure, particularly at that moment in history. Designed by French architect Gustave Eiffel and completed in March 1889, the tower was not only Paris' premiere landmark. It was also the beloved symbol of France and the French people. Hoffmann's pictures of the tower and Hitler together would immediately be distributed across the globe. They would send a powerful message to all who saw them: Nazi Germany had triumphed over one of its main opponents in the ongoing war.

Most people who looked at the photos, Hitler knew,

They would send a powerful message to all who saw them: Nazi Germany had triumphed over one of its main opponents in the ongoing war.

France's beloved symbol, the Eiffel Tower, looms behind Hitler and his senior staff.

would probably draw a second conclusion as well: With France at its knees, Germany would almost certainly invade Britain next. If that last major bastion of the formerly free Europe fell, Hitler would be a huge step closer to his ultimate goal. It was nothing less than world domination.

Not surprisingly, therefore, the photos greatly boosted the morale of the German people. One of the photos of Hitler walking with his officers in front of the Eiffel Tower appeared in the July 1, 1940, issue of one of Germany's biggest newspapers, the *Rheinische Landeszeitung*.

It was like the proverbial icing on the cake for the millions of elated Germans who had read in the paper a few days before: "German people! Your soldiers have in just under six weeks fought a heroic battle in the west. ... Their deeds will go down in history as the greatest victory of all time! We thank God for this victory." For two painful decades, Germans had felt shame and anger over losing World War I to France, Britain, and the other Allies. Now, however, many of them felt they were back where they belonged—at the center of the world stage.

Hitler's enemies viewed the photos very differently. The French were quite naturally crushed and disturbed that Hitler's armies had overrun their country. Yet some of the French refused to knuckle under. And Hoffmann's photo of Hitler standing before the Eiffel Tower inspired the members of the French underground who were mobilizing to fight to liberate their homeland. Across the English Channel, meanwhile, the British, who knew full well they were next on Hitler's hit list, also prepared to fight.

On the other side of the Atlantic, Americans were no less disheartened and disturbed by the same photos. President Franklin D. Roosevelt had for some time been urging Congress to approve sending aid to America's European allies.

British Prime Minister Winston Churchill had made a direct appeal for help during a June 4 speech to the House of Commons. In it he warned of the possible fall of France and the possibility of Britain's having to stand alone against

SHOULD PARIS BE DESTROYED?

Albert Speer (left), a member of Hitler's inner circle, inspects building plans with the Nazi leader.

On the evening before their whirlwind trip to Paris, Albert Speer arrived at Hitler's headquarters in Belgium. Having summoned his favorite architect, Hitler welcomed him. Speer's recollections of the meeting speak volumes about Hitler's feelings about the French capital.

"He was sitting alone at a table," Speer later wrote. "Without much ado he declared: 'Draw up a decree in my name ordering full-scale resumption of work on the Berlin buildings. ... Wasn't Paris beautiful? But Berlin must be made far more beautiful. In the past I often considered whether we would not have to destroy Paris,' he continued with great calm, as if he were talking about the most natural thing in the world. 'But when we are finished in Berlin, Paris will only be a shadow. So why should we destroy it?' With that, I was dismissed."

The pictures reminded them that Hitler was a threat to human liberty who must be resisted and defeated at all costs.

the Germans. If that happened, he said, "We shall fight on the beaches, we shall fight on the landing grounds, we shall fight in the fields and in the streets, we shall fight in the hills. We shall never surrender!"

In his appeal to the U.S. to join the fight against the Nazis, Churchill said the British would carry on "until, in God's good time, the new world, with all its power and might, steps forth to the rescue and the liberation of the old."

When Hoffmann's photos of France's fall reached the United States, they quickly became evidence to strengthen the president's argument. Britain would surely be the Nazis' next target, he declared, and the British badly needed American help. "The people of Europe who are defending themselves do not ask us to do their fighting," Roosevelt said. "They ask us for the implements of war, the planes, the tanks, the guns, the freighters which will enable them to fight for their liberty and for our security." With gusto, he added, "We must get these weapons to them."

The calls for help were eventually heeded. Beginning early in 1941, the United States sent enormous amounts of weapons and supplies overseas in the Lend-Lease program. Hoffmann's photos hadn't intimidated the world. Instead of terrorizing his opponents, the pictures reminded them that Hitler was a threat to human liberty who must be resisted and defeated at all costs.

ChapterFour
REMINDERS OF THE DARK FORCES

The pictures Heinrich Hoffmann snapped in Paris in 1940 were not the first or last he took of Adolf Hitler and the events of World War II. But today they are among the most recognizable of the tens of millions of photos taken during that conflict. Indeed, Hoffmann turned out to be one of the chief German photographic chroniclers of the war.

He seemed to sense the crucial role he had played in capturing the conflict for posterity. In 1955 he said he hoped that members of "future generations that were not there to live through it" would benefit from "some truly historical photographs" he had taken during the war. He hoped they would learn something from these "ghostly transfixed fragments of history perpetuated by a man named Heinrich Hoffmann."

Thus, Hoffmann's professional legacy consisted of a group of pictures that documented important historical events. Most people see the legacy as largely positive. Of course, his employer's legacy was decidedly negative. In fact, Hitler is universally viewed as one of the most despicable people in history. The striking differences between the two men can be seen in the dissimilar ways their final years transpired.

For Adolf Hitler, the photos of him standing before the Eiffel Tower marked his high point of power and pride. In the years after his capture of France, his fortunes for the

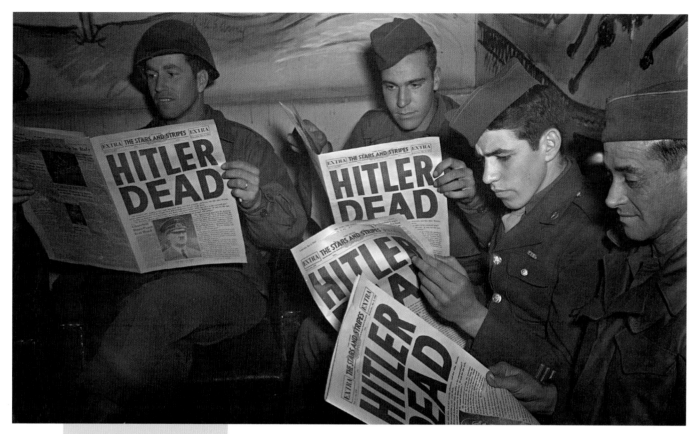

American soldiers read the news of Adolf Hitler's April 30 suicide in the military newspaper, *The Stars and Stripes.*

most part spiraled downward.

He was unable to seize Britain, as he had planned to do. Then the Allies steadily surrounded Germany. The British and Americans advanced from the west and the Russians from the east. Despite occasional successes, the German army had one defeat after another.

In spring 1945 the vast outburst of death and destruction known as World War II finally ended in Europe. Hitler's promise to lead the Germans to greatness had turned to scorching ashes in their mouths. The Führer, now revealed as a false messiah, committed suicide in a concrete bunker deep beneath Berlin's rubble-strewn streets.

In the months that followed, the scale of the destruction Hitler had caused became frighteningly evident. Berlin and other German cities lay in ruins. Worse, more than 50 million people had died worldwide. Among them were at least 11 million Jews, Slavs, Gypsies, and others whom Hitler had declared inferior. The Nazis had systematically murdered them in cold blood using firing squads, gas chambers, starvation, and other means.

These and other heinous acts gave Hitler an unequalled reputation for brutality and cruelty. His very name conjures up many unflattering images. In historian John Toland's words, they include "a madman, a political and military bungler, an evil murderer beyond redemption whose successes were reached by criminal means."

Hitler's photographer emerged from the most devastating war in history with a far less tarnished reputation. Hoffmann was arrested by U.S. authorities at the conflict's close. This was to be expected. After all, he had been a close confidant of the German dictator. Hoffmann was also tried in court and convicted of profiting from the war. Most of his money was taken away, and he was sentenced to 10 years in prison, although he did not serve the full term.

When he was released from prison in May 1950, Hoffmann felt exhausted. The fast-paced job of being Hitler's photographer had a taken a toll on him. So had the distress caused by the trial and imprisonment. He wanted only to settle down and lead a quiet life. "Mentally, I

The fast-paced job of being Hitler's photographer had a taken a toll on him.

confess I have had enough," he said. "I want no more experiences. I need no new impulses. I am content to sit back in peace."

Hoffmann sought that peace in a small house in a village not far from Munich. In his last years, he took no more photos. His most taxing activity was to write his memories of being Hitler's photographer. The book, *Hitler Was My Friend,* was published in 1955. Its author died two years later, of natural causes, at age 72.

A FACE IN THE CROWD

Historians believe Hoffmann doctored a photo to show Hitler attending a 1914 rally.

Did Heinrich Hoffmann take a photo of Adolf Hitler years before they met without realizing it? Many people thought so, but now that assertion is coming under fire.

Supposedly the photo was taken at the moment the German people heard that their country had entered World War I. Thousands of people had gathered in a Munich public square that day—August 2, 1914. Most were excited at the news. Hoffmann was there and snapped shots of the crowd. Fifteen years passed, the story goes. In 1929 Hitler casually told Hoffmann he had been in that crowd. Hoffmann hurried to his lab and found the negative. Sure enough, buried in the multitude of smiling people was a face with a distinctive mustache. Hoffmann was certain it belonged to Hitler, then 25 and unknown to most Germans.

The photo is intriguing. But several historians have questioned its authenticity. They suspect that Hoffmann later inserted Hitler's face into the picture for propaganda purposes. Although Hoffmann supposedly found the picture in 1929, he didn't publish it until 1932, when Hitler's patriotism was being questioned.

"No other photographer in history landed the scoop that he did."

Though Hoffmann was gone, his legacy remained. He was "one of the most important photographers of the 20th century," said British historian Roger Moorhouse. "No other photographer in history landed the scoop that he did." He had gotten "exclusive access to a major head of state. And importantly," he had had "the chance to work with a subject who knew very well how to 'work' the camera." Indeed, Moorhouse said, Hitler "paid painstaking attention to the cultivation of his public image." In that regard Hoffmann, more than anyone else, "shaped Hitler's public image and charted the rise of the Third Reich. Hoffmann's pictures of the Führer were sold worldwide, used for newspapers, magazines, postcards, placards and posters, even postage stamps. His pictures were … adored in countless German homes, just as they were often vilified abroad."

Many British, French, Americans, and other opponents of Nazi Germany at first denounced Hoffmann for taking the pictures. They associated him directly with Hitler. They assumed that the photographer must have approved of the war crimes Hitler committed. Even decades after Hoffmann's death, his "significance as a photographer" was "still overshadowed by his close connection to Hitler," Moorhouse said.

This view of Hoffmann may not be fully accurate. Hoffmann said he did not know about all of the Nazi abuses. Moreover, he said he did not approve of the ones he did know about. And even though he was a longtime member of the Nazi Party, he said he did not care about or follow Nazi ideals.

Hoffmann saw Hitler very differently than nearly all other Germans did. To him, his boss was basically a man in a high position who liked him and gave him an outlet for his photographic skills. "With Hitler, the Führer and Chancellor of the Third Reich, I have but little concern," Hoffmann said in his 1955 book. "But Adolf Hitler, the man, was my friend." He "returned my friendship and gave me his complete confidence; he looms large in the tale of my life."

Moorhouse said the photographer's explanation was correct. "Hoffmann does not come across as a political animal," Moorhouse wrote. "It seems clear that his relationship with Hitler was one that was born primarily out of a personal, rather than an ideological, affinity."

Moorhouse characterizes Hoffmann's memories as "rosy." Hoffmann's book, he said, recounts "life seen from the perspective of the blinkered, cosseted inner circle of the Third Reich, with no hint of the darkness, corruption and horror that the regime propagated elsewhere."

Hoffmann offered no regrets for his actions. "One must infer," wrote Moorhouse, "that he did not feel that he had done anything for which to apologize." And whatever people thought about Hoffmann in the past, or will in the future, one thing about him is certain: The size and importance of his body of work are undeniable.

The U.S. military seized much of his enormous collection of pictures in 1945. Included were the shots

Russian photographer Sergey Larenkov uses Hoffmann's famous photo to "penetrate the layers of time," as he puts it. He superimposes the Paris image on a modern photo of the same view for a link to the past.

of Hitler in Paris posing before the Eiffel Tower. The confiscated photos are now in the National Archives in Washington, D.C. The collection is a major source of images for historians studying the Third Reich and for publishers of books about Hitler and the Nazis.

The pictures are in the public domain. That means that no one owns the rights to them, so anyone can use them for free. As their creator, Hoffmann originally owned them, and under normal circumstances, his estate would still own them. But when the U.S. government seized them as Nazi property, those rights vanished.

The Library of Congress in Washington, D.C., holds many of Hoffmann's photos of Hitler in its Third Reich Collection.

Another large collection of Hoffmann's photos is in the Bavarian State Library in Munich. Smaller collections of Hoffmann's pictures also probably exist. In January 2011 a British auction house sold more than 600 Hoffmann photos for the equivalent of nearly $48,000. The family of a man described only as elderly put the pictures up for auction. Supposedly Hoffmann had given the photos to the man in the 1940s. According to the auctioneer, Jonathan Humbert, they provide "a sinister but intriguing social history of the rise of the Nazi Party, never before ... seen."

Wherever they may rest today, Hoffmann's photos will surely long remain valuable historical documents. They provide a primary and priceless insight into one of history's darkest and most far-reaching episodes. Of his many stunning shots, those showing Hitler in Paris continue to stand out. They are potent reminders that brutal dictators such as Hitler always lurk in the shadows. If given the chance, they are ready to unleash the dark forces of hate and intolerance on the unwary and unprepared. The peoples of the world must remain ever on their guard.

Timeline

1885

Heinrich Hoffmann, who will become Hitler's personal photographer, is born in the Germanic kingdom of Bavaria

1889

Adolf Hitler, the future dictator of Germany, is born in Austria

1908

Hitler applies to the Vienna Arts Academy but is rejected

1920

Hitler helps to establish the renamed National Socialist German Workers Party—the Nazi Party

1923

The Nazis attempt a coup against the government of Bavaria, but the takeover fails and Hitler is jailed

1914–1918

World War I, known as the war to end all wars, is fought

1919

Germany signs the Treaty of Versailles with the Allies (led by France, Britain, and the United States)

1930

The Nazi Party wins 107 seats in Germany's parliament in a national election

1933

Hitler is appointed chancellor of Germany and almost immediately turns the country into a police state

Timeline

1934

More than 1 million people attend a Nazi rally at Nuremberg

1936

Hitler signs a nonaggression pact with Italy's dictator, Benito Mussolini

1939

German forces invade Poland, starting World War II

1947

Hoffmann is tried and convicted of war profiteering

1950

Hoffmann is released from prison and settles in a village near Munich

1940

France falls to Germany, and Hitler visits Paris, where Hoffmann takes several iconic photos of him

1945

World War II ends with Germany's utter defeat; Hitler marries Eva Braun; both commit suicide; Hoffmann is arrested and imprisoned

1955

Hoffmann's book *Hitler Was My Friend* is published

1957

Hoffmann dies of natural causes

Glossary

adulation: intense praise or reverence

anti-Semitism: prejudice or discrimination against Jewish people

armistice: formal agreement to end the fighting during a war

degenerate: person who has sunk to a lower moral level than normal

dictator: ruler who takes complete control of a country, often unjustly

disgruntled: displeased or annoyed

fascist: form of government that promotes extreme nationalism, repression, anticommunism, and is ruled by a dictator

iconic: widely viewed as perfectly capturing the meaning or spirit of something or someone

irrational: illogical or absurd

nonentity: unimportant person

onslaught: major attack

posterity: future ages and generations

propaganda: information spread to try to influence the thinking of people; often not completely true or fair

signature: distinctive mark or characteristic indicating identity

swastika: cross with the ends of its four arms bent into right angles; originally an ancient religious symbol, it was used as an emblem of the Nazi Party and Germany during Hitler's rule

Third Reich: official name of the Nazi regime that ruled Germany from 1933 to 1945

tuberculosis: lung disease that causes fever, coughing, and difficulty breathing

uncanny: strange or mysterious

Additional Resources

Further Reading

Barber, Nicola. *Churchill and the Battle of Britain.*
Chicago: Capstone Heinemann Library, 2013.

Freeman, Charles. *Why Did the Rise of the Nazis Happen?*
New York: Gareth Stevens Pub., 2011.

Layton, Geoff. *From Kaiser to Fuhrer: Germany 1900–1945.*
London: Hodder Education, 2009.

Price, Sean. *Adolf Hitler.* New York: Franklin Watts, 2010.

Stille, Darlene R. *Architects of the Holocaust.*
Mankato, Minn.: Compass Point Books, 2010.

Internet Sites

Use FactHound to find Internet sites related
to this book. All of the sites on FactHound
have been researched by our staff.

Here's all you do:
Visit *www.facthound.com*
Type in this code: 9780756547332

Critical Thinking Using the Common Core

What are two reasons that Adolf Hitler wanted to have photos of himself standing before the Eiffel Tower? How did Germany's adversaries react to the photos? (Key Ideas and Details)

Look at the photo of Adolf Hitler on page 8. How do you think it might have been used in an attempt to show him as beloved by the German people? (Craft and Structure)

What are three of Heinrich Hoffmann's notable accomplishments as a 20th century photographer, as discussed on pages 28 and 51? Explain what Hoffmann believed made his photos distinct. (Key Ideas and Details)

Source Notes

Page 4, line 20: Heinrich Hoffmann. *Hitler Was My Friend.* Yorkshire, England: Pen and Sword, 2011, p. vii.

Page 4, line 23: Ibid.

Page 7, line 1: Ibid, p. 46.

Page 7, line 8: Ibid. p. 134.

Page 9, line 7: Robert G.L. Waite. *The Psychopathic God: Adolf Hitler.* New York: Da Capo Press, 1993, p. 3.

Page 10, line 21: William L. Shirer. *The Rise and Fall of the Third Reich: A History of Nazi Germany.* New York: Simon and Schuster, 1960, p. 49

Page 14, line 8: Steven Heller. *"Heinrich Hoffmann: Adolf Hitler's Personal Lichtbildner and Publicist,"* p.35. 30 Sept. 2013. http://www. hellerbooks.com/pdfs/baseline_ heinrich_hoffmann.pdf

Page 15, line 7: William L. Shirer. *Berlin Diary: The Journal of a Foreign Correspondent, 1934-1941.* New York: A.A. Knopf, 1941, pp. 16–18.

Page 19, line 1: John Toland. *Adolf Hitler.* Garden City, N.Y.: Doubleday, 1976, p. 27.

Page 20, line 18: "Hitler's First Major Statement on Anti-Semitism: Reply to Adolf Gemlich (September 16, 1919)." German History in Documents and Images. 30 Sept. 2013. http:// germanhistorydocs.ghi-dc.org/docpage. cfm?docpage_id=4809

Page 20, line 28: *The Rise and Fall of the Third Reich: A History of Nazi Germany,* p. 54.

Page 22, line 15: Crane Brinton et al. *A History of Civilization, 1815 to the Present.* Englewood Cliffs, N.J.: Prentice-Hall, 1976, p. 759.

Page 25, line 2: Winston S. Churchill. *The Gathering Storm.* Boston: Houghton Mifflin, 1948, pp. 189–190.

Page 26, line 6: *The Rise and Fall of the Third Reich: A History of Nazi Germany,* p. 738.

Page 26, line 20: *Hitler Was My Friend,* p. vi.

Page 27, line 7: Ibid., p. 15.

Page 28, line 16: Ibid., p. 33.

Page 28, line 25: Ibid., pp. 26–27.

Page 29, line 8: Ibid., p. 39.

Page 30, line 2: Ibid., p. 39.

Page 30, line 13: Ibid., p. 49.

Page 30, line 18: Ibid., p. 70.

Page 30, line 28: Ibid., p. 71.

Page 31, line 7: *The Psychopathic God: Adolf Hitler,* p. 41.

Page 35, line 1: *Hitler Was My Friend,* p. 121.

Page 36, line 16: Ibid., p. 122.

Page 36, line 25: Ibid.

Page 37, line 6: *The Rise and Fall of the Third Reich: A History of Nazi Germany,* p. 742.

Page 39, line 4: Albert Speer. *Inside the Third Reich.* New York: Macmillan, 1970, p. 204.

Page 39, line 7: Ibid.

Page 39, line 21: *Hitler Was My Friend,* p. 122.

Page 39, line 24: Ibid.

Page 43, line 3: "The War in the West has Ended." *Rheinische Landeszeitung.* 25 June 1940, p. 1.

Page 44, line 6: *Inside the Third Reich,* pp. 206–207.

Page 45, line 1: BBC History "Fight on the beaches" 30 Sept. 2013. http:// www.bbc.co.uk/history/topics/fight_ on_the_beaches

Page 45, line 14: Fireside Chat 16: On the "Arsenal of Democracy." 29 Dec. 1940. 30 Sept. 2013. Miller Center, University of Virginia. http:// millercenter.org/president/speeches/ detail/3319

Page 46, line 9: *Hitler Was My Friend,* p. 250.

Page 48, line 12: *Adolf Hitler,* p. xiii.

Page 48, line 28: *Hitler Was My Friend,* p. 248.

Page 51, line 2: Ibid, p. 11.

Page 51, line 11: Ibid, p. 9.

Page 51, line 22: Ibid, p. 10.

Page 52, line 6: Ibid, p. 16.

Page 52, line 13: Ibid, p. 14.

Page 55, line 9: "Hundreds of Hitler pictures from his personal photographer brought to light and put up for auction." *Mail Online.* 29 Nov. 2010. 30 Sept. 2013. http://www. dailymail.co.uk/news/article-1333831/ Hundreds-Hitler-pictures-personal- photographer-brought-light-auction. html#ixzz2XR1iMU1M

Select Bibliography

Brinton, Crane, et al. *A History of Civilization, 1815 to the Present*. Englewood Cliffs, N.J.: Prentice-Hall, 1976.

Churchill, Winston S. *The Gathering Storm*. Boston: Houghton Mifflin, 1948.

Crew, David F. *Hitler and the Nazis: A History in Documents*. New York: Oxford University Press, 2005.

Davidson, Eugene. *The Making of Adolf Hitler: The Birth and Rise of Nazism*. Columbia: University of Missouri Press, 1997.

Feuchtwanger, E.J. *From Weimar to Hitler: Germany, 1918–33*. New York: St. Martin's Press, 2004.

Grunberger, Richard. *The 12-Year Reich: A Social History of Nazi Germany, 1933–1945*. New York: De Capo Press, 1995.

Hitler, Adolf. *Mein Kampf*. Trans. Ralph Manheim. Boston: Houghton Mifflin, 1971.

Hoffmann, Heinrich. *Hitler Was My Friend*. Yorkshire, England: Pen and Sword, 2011.

Jackson, Julian. *The Fall of France: The Nazi Invasion of 1940*. New York: Oxford University Press, 2004.

Kershaw, Ian. *Hitler, 1889-1936: Hubris*. New York: W.W. Norton, 2000.

Kershaw, Ian. *Hitler, 1936-1945: Nemesis*. New York: W.W. Norton, 2001.

Noakes, Jeremy, and Geoffrey Pridham, eds. *Documents on Nazism, 1919-1945*. New York: Viking Press, 1990.

Shirer, William L. *Berlin Diary: The Journal of a Foreign Correspondent, 1934–1941*. New York: A.A. Knopf, 1941.

Shirer, William L. *The Rise and Fall of the Third Reich: A History of Nazi Germany*. New York: Simon and Schuster, 1960.

Snyder, Louis L. *The War: A Concise History, 1939–1945*. New York: Dell, 1964.

Speer, Albert. *Inside the Third Reich*. New York: Macmillan, 1970.

Spielvogel, Jackson J. *Hitler and Nazi Germany: A History*. Boston.: Prentice-Hall, 2010.

Toland, John. *Adolf Hitler*. Garden City, N.Y.: Doubleday, 1976.

Waite, Robert G.L. *The Psychopathic God: Adolf Hitler*. New York: Da Capo Press, 1993.

Welch, David. *The Third Reich: Politics and Propaganda*. London: Routledge, 2002.

Index

About the Author

Historian and award-winning author Don Nardo has written many books for young people about American history and world history. Nardo lives with his wife, Christine, in Massachusetts.